Home
Candle Making

Easy Ideas for Making & Gifting
Artisan-Inspired Candles

Stephanie Rose

LEISURE ARTS, INC. • Maumelle, Arkansas

Introduction

I live in a wonderful neighborhood. Every year the families on our block get together at one of the houses for a festive holiday celebration. When it was my turn to host, I simply set out glasses, cutlery and plates and made room at the table for the communal potluck meal. It was an easy task and I didn't expect any of the neighbors to bring me a gift in addition to what they were contributing to the potluck.

But, of course, many of them did.

At the end of the night, I ended up with quite a number of bottles of wine (which I certainly did not mind) and one cinnamon-scented red candle, set on top of a wood slice and wrapped in golden cellophane.

When my crafty neighbor presented me with this exquisite candle, I enthusiastically expressed that I didn't expect gifts, and shouldn't accept such a beautiful (and clearly expensive) one. She said, "Oh, please take it! I love making candles. It's such fun for me to do and I would love to give you one to enjoy."

Well, I stopped arguing right there. As a lifelong creative person, I know firsthand how much joy comes from making homemade gifts. I gleefully accepted the candle and set it alight for the whole party to enjoy.

When I started making candles, I was pleasantly surprised at how easy it was to make absolutely gorgeous handcrafted creations that looked like they

came from a boutique. The more candles I made, the more methods I tried, and it quickly became a way for me to relax doing a hobby that fulfilled my creative spirit. I offered to make candles for friends and family for events and even wedding favors. I started giving candles instead of hostess gifts and you wouldn't believe how many more dinner invitations I received. Having the opportunity to make something handmade gives you an opportunity to play. To be creative. To make something wonderful. And to spend your time well. I would much rather head out to the craft room and make something that I can give as a gift than shop for something much less personal.

My hope is that what you find on these pages will bring you joy as well; feeding your creative spirit while stocking your shelves with heartfelt gifts. This book will help you explore a number of different artisan-inspired candle projects that can be easily replicated at home. Not only that, but they'll suit many different occasions, from housewarmings to weddings to pick-me-up gifts. Once you are finished crafting each stunning candle, I'll provide suggestions for how to wrap each one. The combination allows you to truly make and give something special.

 To Charlie, Tavish, and Asher:
three sparks that light up the world.

Contents

Projects

About Candles

There are many different types of candles: container candles, votives, pillars, tapers, and more. Some techniques require years of practice and special equipment, but there are also candles that are simple to make at home. With easy access to the three essential ingredients for a candle – wax, wicks and fragrance – there is no reason why even a beginner candle maker can't handcraft magnificent projects right in their kitchen. This book showcases a number of techniques for how to make container candles and wax melts, using both equipment and supplies that are readily available at craft stores and online.

CONTAINER CANDLES

Making container candles allows for a great deal of creativity because you can customize so many parts of the process: melting wax, adding color and fragrance, pouring it into a heatproof container and adding a wick. If a container is in the appropriate shape to hold a candle, and it is made of a material that can withstand the heat of molten wax, then you can probably make a candle in it! A few other considerations like volume and shape will help you to make the best container candle.

Container volume – a candle can be made in a small container or a large container, you will only need to adjust the amount of wax and number of wicks needed. A small candle is a wonderful use of expensive materials like beeswax and essential oils, while a large candle will require a lot more materials. Large candles will also need multiple wicks to burn the candle to the edges.

Container shape – flames need oxygen, so the container should have a wide opening to allow for proper air exposure. Containers that widen below the neck of a smaller opening may not burn evenly and can produce excessive smoke.

WAX MELTS

A wax melt is a scented square of wax that can be melted in an electric- or candle-heated ceramic warmer to release the wax scent. Wax melts are a way to get all of the fragrance and warmth of a candle without the flame.

The beauty of wax melts is that you can use botanicals and dry herbs to decorate your projects without the worry of them catching fire. The electric options also keep your home safe from flames if you have young children or pets.

GIFT WRAP

The candles you create will be undoubtedly gorgeous, so they won't need much extra to make them a special gift. Even so, by adding some jute twine, a label or some fabric, your candles will be dressed to highlight their craftsmanship, while celebrating their purpose as gifts.

CANDLE SAFETY

Candles are a wonderful way to add natural light and fragrance, but they are also no joke when it comes to fire safety. Homemade candles should never be burned unattended, just like any candle. Keep them out of the path of children and pets and never add things near the flame like glitter or herbs that can spark and float into the air. Be prepared to extinguish the candle by covering it with a candle snuffer. Do not throw water on a candle to extinguish it and don't touch the melted wax or move the candle with melted wax while it is still liquid to prevent splatters, spills, and burns. Please always use your common sense with any DIY project, especially when fire is involved.

WICKS

Wicks come in many different materials and forms, from basic cotton on a roll to wired and waxed wicks with tabs. No matter which you choose, you need the right size (thickness) for your candle to burn properly. Wicks that are too small will not melt the wax all the way to the edge of the candle, creating a tunnel in the center. Wicks that are too large will create a lot of smoke. (Although both of the aforementioned situations are also used as techniques in projects in this book.) Look for labeling on the package of wicks to see what wax and candle diameter they are appropriate for.

Tips

Keep wicks trimmed to ⅛" to ¼" for best results. Be sure to only trim the wicks once the candles have fully cooled and cured for 24 hours.

- Cotton wicks come as a roll of cotton string that has been braided to provide thickness.

- Wired wicks have a thin zinc wire in the center that helps to hold the wick straight.

- Waxed wicks are coated with wax. If you are making a paraffin coated candle, use a paraffin coated wick. If you are making a soy or beeswax candle, use a soy wax-coated wick (a soy wax-coated wick has proven to perform better than a beeswax-coated wick in a beeswax candle).

- Wood wicks are flat wicks made of soft wood that sound like a crackling fire when they burn. Wood wicks do not need trimming after they are burned.

- Tabs are metal disks (or, in the case of wood wicks, they are rectangular) that weigh the wick down and give you a place to glue the wick to the bottom of the container (if appropriate).

SCENT

Candle scent is differentiated by hot throw (the scent that a candle gives off when burned) and cold throw (the scent that an unlit candle gives off). Both essential oils and fragrance oils can be used to scent your candles, however, you may choose one or the other based on the following factors.

Fragrance oils offer the most consistent and reliable scent. They have been formulated to be heated to high temperatures and added to molten wax without evaporation. Fragrance oils also come in a wide-variety of lab-created scents like strawberry and green apple that are pleasing and not available as essential oils.

Essential oils are natural scents extracted from plants and they are sometimes better tolerated by people with scent sensitivities or allergies. Essential oils are used in aromatherapy with different healing effects (such as relaxation or focus) being ascribed to the aromatic diffusion. Essential oils typically have expected cold throw but can be inconsistent with hot throw as each oil type and oil manufacturer will produce oils with differing qualities. This is because some essential oils will evaporate at the high temperatures needed for binding the scent with the wax. When the candle cools, the scent could evaporate and leave the candle with very little scent.

Fragrance load is how much scent oil the wax will hold. A common fragrance load for soy wax is one ounce of scent oil per one pound of wax or a 6.25% ratio.

You can increase or decrease the ratio depending on how strong the scent is. Use 8-10% for a subtly fragrant oil and 6-8% for a strongly scented one.

When you are starting out, using the one-ounce-per-pound-of-wax rule is both easy to measure and a safe bet that the candle will turn out well. After 7% fragrance load, some candles can have issues with wicking. Be sure to check the maximum on the wax you are using if you plan to go higher.

To calculate how much scent oil is needed, use this formula: (oz of wax) x (% scent oil) = (oz of scent oil needed).

Candle-Making Temperature

Color and scent are added at a higher temperature than you will pour the candle at. The temperature differs depending on what type of wax you are using as they have differing melt points. Soy wax will melt somewhere between 120°F and 180°F depending on the blend. The packaging or instructions should list both the temperature to add color and scent, as well as the temperature to pour the wax. For example, using a basic container blend of soy wax flakes, you would add the fragrance and color when the wax reaches 160°F and stir thoroughly for one minute. Then cool the wax to a lower temperature between 140°F and 150°F to pour it. Adding the scent oil and dye at the right time ensures that it will properly bind to the wax and be evenly distributed. Pouring at the right temperature ensures you will have the best looking candles by preventing a host of problems.

Getting Started

The projects in this book show many methods of crafting candles in different styles but the basic steps for making container candles and wax melts are generally the same, no matter what wax, wicks or containers you use. Follow these basic steps to make a simple container candle, then visit the projects to get ideas for how to craft and wrap up something personal and creative.

Select an appropriate container for your candle. Any heatproof container that is clean and free from cracks or holes is a good choice. Some choices are glass canning jars, glass candle holders, metal tins, ceramic tea or coffee cups, and seashells.

If required, assemble the wick so that it has a metal tab on the bottom. For a cotton wick, thread it through the hole in the metal tab and clamp the hole shut using pliers. Trim the excess wick from the bottom of the tab so that it sits flat in the bottom of the container.

Add the wick to the container with a dab of hot glue or wax adhesive on the bottom of the tab. Press it firmly to the bottom center of the container. If you can't reach your fingers into the container, use a straw or a pen casing with the ink removed to press it down firmly.

Assemble a double boiler by filling the bottom pot with a few inches of water and reserving the inner pot for melting the wax. If using wax blocks, cut them into smaller pieces before melting.

Weigh the required amount of wax on a kitchen scale by zeroing the scale with the inner part of the double boiler on the scale and then adding the wax.

Weigh the required amount of fragrance or essential oil using a kitchen scale. Small paper cups or shot glasses make a perfect tool for this! Set the fragrance or essential oil aside.

Heat the wax over medium heat until the wax is completely melted and reaches the temperature indicated in the recipe or on the packaging from the wax you have purchased.

If you are adding color and scent, bring the temperature up to the temperature specified on the wax packaging (i.e.: 160°F) for adding dye and scent oil. (See **Candle-Making Temperature** on page 11.)

Remove the wax from the heat and stir the dye in until it is completely dissolved. The amount of dye you need per pound of wax will be listed on the package of wax dye, or you can blend until you like the hue, keeping in mind it will change when the candle is dry. To determine the final wax color, place a spoonful of wax in paper cup of cold water. It will dry quickly and when you remove the wax from the water, you will see the final color.

Tips, Tricks & Troubleshooting

In candle making, there are a few issues that might arise with the appearance, burning or scent. This list of tips and tricks can help to troubleshoot any problems you may run into with your candle projects.

- In many cases, pouring container candles in two steps is not necessary, but it can also depend on the wax you use and varying room and wax temperature. If you get a depressed area around the wick when cooled, warm up some more wax and pour a thin layer of wax on top of the candle to smooth out the surface.

- You can also smooth out the top surface of a candle using a low temperature heat gun. Do not try using a blow dryer as it will melt and splatter the wax.

- Some brands of soy wax can create dimples when burned, giving the candle a less attractive appearance. If this happens, consider using a soy wax blend or using a different brand of soy wax.

- Cracks in the candle can happen if the wax was cooled too quickly or left in a cold room.

- Use a soft cloth to buff the surface of your candle to give it a smooth appearance.

- Heat the container on a candle warming pad before pouring the candle and cool it slowly to prevent "wet spots".

- Use the right sized wick and keep it trimmed to 1/4" long to avoid excess smokiness.

- If the wick disappears into the pool of wax, the wick diameter may be too small for the candle. Use a larger diameter wick next time.

- The right size wick is one that will allow the candle wax to burn all the way to the edges without being too large, which would cause the candle to smoke. Test a different size wick to see if that improves the results.

- Most of the wicks are chosen based on the type of wax you're using. But it turns out that a soy wax-coated wick will work just as well in beeswax as it will in soy wax. If you're using paraffin wax, then it's essential to use wicks made for paraffin wax.

- If the candle scent isn't as strong as you would like it, use a reliable brand of scent oil created for candle making. Adding more candle scent than the recipe calls for may end up being too much oil for the wax to bind with, leaving you with excess oil at the surface and bottom of the candle.

- Pour leftover wax into a silicone cupcake or soap mold to cool. The puck-shaped wax will be easy to melt the next time you want to make candles.

- Wipe wax from containers and utensils using a paper towel while the wax is still warm. Once the wax sets, it is much more difficult to clean off the equipment. Do not pour wax down the drain.

- When adding anything into a candle other than wax, wicks, scent oils, and dyes made for candle making, be aware that it could catch on fire. If you add herbs or other elements like glitter, color or even essential oils to a candle, they can react in a way that you might not expect.

All candles should never be burned without you in attendance. Always be prepared to extinguish a candle by covering it. Do not throw water on a burning candle as it can cause the wax to splatter.

The Projects

Now that you have the basics of candle making, it's time to fire up your creative ideas! The following pages show how many different ways candles can be created using wax, wicks and containers. The projects have themes that incorporate the container, the scent and even the giftwrap that work together for gift-giving. There's a coffee candle for co-workers, jam jar candles for wedding favors and citronella candles for a garden party.

When you head out to gather the supplies you can easily swap out elements to make the projects your own. Customize each candle with your favorite scents, colors and containers so that they suit your personal style.

But I should warn you, once you start making some of these candle projects you'll look at containers in a whole different way. Common things around you will all become potential vessels for your latest candle creations!

How wonderful is it to use candles to repurpose an unused object and display a treasure? An empty jar may be rescued from the recycling bin. A favorite mug could get an honorary spot on the kitchen table. And found souvenirs like seashells can help to light up some memories and the night.

Cappuccino Candle

MAKES ONE 8 OZ (225 G) CANDLE

It's likely that you have a few unused coffee cups lying around the house. There are so many stylish coffee cups out there, it's easy to buy one every time you visit a store. Before you know it, you have more mugs than you know what to do with. Here is what to do with them: make a coffee candle! These coffee-scented cappuccino candles have an invigorating (and yummy) aroma and they make a great gift for the coworkers and coffee-lovers in your life.

MATERIALS

- One 4" bowl-shaped coffee cup with a wide mouth
- 8 oz (225 g) of soy wax for container candles
- One wood wick and metal tab
- 0.8 oz (24 ml) coffee fragrance or essential oil

EQUIPMENT

- Double boiler
- Hot glue gun and glue or wax adhesive
- Thermometer
- Old towel
- Fine-tip pruning shears to cut wick
- Kitchen scale
- Paper cup
- Heatproof container with pour spout

TIP

Customize the color of the candle to match your pal's favorite coffee. Leave the soy wax natural to match the white foam of a cappuccino or add brown wax dye to change the color of the candle to the warm tone of coffee with cream.

Wake up and Smell the Coffee

Research shows that it's not just the caffeine in coffee that wakes you up, but the aroma of coffee also has the power to add cheer and energy to your day. So, if you are trying to kick the caffeine habit, or just want a little extra pep in your step, light up this coffee-scented candle.

1 Weigh the soy wax and add it to a double boiler on medium heat. While the wax is melting, measure the scent oil into a paper cup.

2 Prepare the wood wick by measuring the final height in the cup, ¼" above the final top of the wax; cut the wick. Feed the wooden wick into the metal base and use a dab of hot glue or wax adhesive to attach it to the bottom of the cup at the center.

3 When the melted wax has reached the specified temperature for adding dye or scent oil (i.e.: 160°F – see the instructions that came with your wax), add the scent oil and wax dye if using. Stir well to bind.

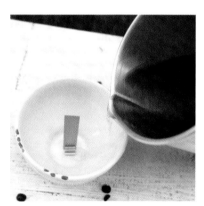

4 Cool the wax to 140°F and pour it into the cup. Wrap the candle in a towel and place it in a warm room to slowly set.

5 Allow your candle to cure for 48 hours undisturbed. Once cured, trim the wick with fine tip pruning shears if it is more than $1/4$" above the wax.

Pair the candle up with a bag of gourmet roasted coffee beans or a gift card to a favorite café for a coffee-themed gift. Add a cute tag that reads, "I like you a Latte," "Thanks a Latte," or "Words Can't Espresso My Love for You."

Clay Pot Citronella Candles

MAKES THREE 2.5" CLAY POT CANDLES

Nothing ruins a summer party more quickly than unwanted guests like mosquitoes and other biting insects! These clay pot candles not only keep pests away but they also make great summer table decorations.

MATERIALS

- Three 2.5" diameter terra cotta pots
- Electrical tape
- Silicone sealer
- Cork sheet
- 1 lb (450 g) soy wax for container candles
- Three HTP-1312 6" waxed and wired wicks with tabs
- 1 oz. (30 ml) of pure citronella oil
- Water base, non-flammable sealer, such as Mod Podge®
- Disposable foam paintbrush

EQUIPMENT

- Hot glue gun and glue
- Double boiler
- Metal tray to hold pots
- Old towel
- Thermometer
- Sharp scissors to cut wick
- Kitchen scale
- Paper cup
- Chopsticks or clothespins
- Heatproof container with pour spout

TIP

The right size wick will burn a candle all the way to the edges of the container without creating a lot of extra smoke. Using a wick that is considered too large for the container increases the amount of smoke the candle produces. Because these candles are meant to keep pests away and will be burned outdoors, choose a larger wick than would normally be appropriate.

Bug off, Naturally

The citronella scent sends annoying bugs flying in the opposite direction, so these pretty candles are perfect additions to your outdoor table for summer evenings on the patio that you want to enjoy itch free. Ah, the power of nature.

MAKE IT! • CLAY POT CITRONELLA CANDLES

1 Use a foam brush to apply the water base sealer to the inside of each pot. Seal up the hole of each pot by placing a few pieces of electrical tape inside the pot, covering the hole.

2 Flip each pot over and fill the hole with silicone sealer. Cut a cork sheet circle that will fit inside the bottom rim of the pot. Use a hot glue gun to attach the cork to the bottom of the pot once the silicone has completely dried.

3 Melt one pound of soy wax flakes in a double boiler and add a thermometer. While the wax is melting, measure the citronella oil into a paper cup and attach a wick to the inner bottom of each clay pot using hot glue.

4 When the melted wax has reached the specified temperature for adding dye or scent oil (i.e.: 160°F – see the instructions that came with your wax), add the citronella oil. Stir well for one full minute to make sure that the oil is completely mixed into the wax.

5 Set the clay pots on a metal tray to protect your work surface from spills or leaks. Use chopsticks or clothespins to keep the wick upright and straight. Cool the wax to 140°F and pour into each of the pots to ½" from the top.

6 Wrap the candles in a towel and allow to dry completely untouched in a warm room. Allow your candles to cure for 48 hours undisturbed. When the candles are cured, trim the wicks to ¼" above the wax.

A set of three citronella candles placed on a chicken wire basket has the right feel for the outdoors. Paint the pots with water base acrylic paint, add a top coat of sealer and tie cords around the rims to make a thoughtful garden party gift. A checkered towel, burlap ribbon and stamped tag make for a pretty presentation. Not only will these candles light up the night, but they will keep only the desired party guest in attendance.

Citrus Celebration Wax Melts

MAKES TWELVE 0.5 OZ (15 G) WAX MELTS

Citrus celebration wax melts are the perfect housewarming gift. The festive scent is both cheerful and uplifting and will give any home a refreshing, energizing feel. Give a pretty wax warmer along with some homemade citrus wax melts topped with lemon, lime and orange zest. An ice cube mold is the perfect size for these wax melts. You will want to make enough to give away and keep some for yourself, too.

MATERIALS

- 6 oz (170g) soy wax for wax melts
- 0.4 oz (12 ml) citrus blend fragrance or essential oils
- One each: fresh lemon, lime and orange
- Wax dye (optional)

EQUIPMENT

- Double boiler
- Thermometer
- Kitchen scale
- Paper cup
- Heatproof container with a pour spout
- Citrus zester
- Silicone ice cube tray

Celebrate with Citrus!

The bright and cheery aroma of citrus is fresh and lively, but also very calming. Use citrus scented candles and wax melts to make your home smell fresh, clean and welcoming. But don't use a grapefruit scent before a dinner party, because it is said to curb the appetite!

1 Weigh soy wax and scent oil.

2 Set up a small double boiler using a heatproof glass jar to hold the wax and a metal bread pan filled part way with water. Stir the wax frequently until it is fully melted.

3 Use the zester to grate the three fruits and mix the zest together.

4 Bring the wax to the specified temperature for adding dye or scent oil (i.e.: 160°F – see the instructions that came with your wax). Add in scent and color (if using) and stir until completely mixed.

5 If you heated the wax in a canning jar, transfer it to a heatproof container with a pour spout for more accuracy when pouring it into the molds. Pour the wax into a silicone ice cube tray and immediately sprinkle the citrus zest on top of each melt.

6 Allow the wax melts to dry completely before popping them out of the mold for use.

To use: Add one or two wax melts to an electric or tea light wax warmer and enjoy the fragrance.

Fill a small canning jar with citrus wax melts and pair it with a tea light wax warmer. Stack and wrap the jar and the wax warmer with a tea light candle, all tied together with a natural ribbon.

Summer Flowers Floating Candles

MAKES SIX 1 OZ (30G) FLOATING CANDLES

Floating candles are a lovely way to add a little fire to a floral centerpiece and they are surprisingly easy to make using metal tart molds. Made with sweet smelling beeswax, these floral-shaped floating candles will be the buzz of the party.

MATERIALS

- 6 oz (170 g) of beeswax
- Six waxed and wired 1" tea light wicks with tabs
- Six mini metal tart molds
- Large, wide glass vase
- Fresh or artificial flowers

EQUIPMENT

- Double boiler
- Kitchen scale
- Baking sheet
- Kitchen scale
- Heatproof container with pour spout

TIP

When making candles in a container that you eventually want to remove, choose a wax formulated for votives or pillar candles or use a candle release additive to allow the wax to pop out of the mold more easily. In the event that the wax doesn't release, pop the mold in the freezer for ten minutes, then try again. Keep freezing at ten-minute intervals until the candle can be removed. Just be sure not to leave the candle in the freezer for an extended period of time or it may crack.

The Power of Flowers

Flowers are the ultimate pick-me-up. Whether you are giving a bouquet to a loved one, arranging them to brighten up your home or planting them in the garden to attract bees and butterflies, flowers add life, color and joy to any space. Next time you are feeling a bit blue, head out and smell the flowers. It will certainly help to improve the day.

1 Measure and melt the beeswax in a double boiler. Keep a close watch on it so that it can be poured as soon as it's completely liquid.

2 Wipe out the tart molds to be sure the insides are quite clean. Place the tart molds on a baking sheet and place paper under the baking sheet to protect the countertops from spills.

How to Display Floating Candles

Floating candles sit right on the surface of water of a vase, glass, bathtub or even a pond. To create a lavish display, fill a wide vase with freshly-cut flowers and fill it with water to cover the blooms completely. The flowers will look great for a few days submerged in water. For an even longer-lasting display, you can use silk flowers in the water. If the flowers try to float to the surface, pack a bunch of blooms and leaves into the vase then add in a smaller floating glass vase filled with a bit of water to hold the candle.

3 Carefully pour wax into the tart molds, making sure that they stay level and wax doesn't pour over the edges. When pouring a small volume of beeswax at a low temperature, the wax may cool and harden on the side of the pouring container. Put the container in the warm water of the double boiler to re-liquefy as needed.

4 As the wax starts to cool and turn opaque around the edges, place a wick into the center of each one. The wicks are short and should easily stay in place.

5 Let the tarts cool and cure for 24 hours undisturbed, then remove them from the mold. As the tart molds have sharp edges, hold them with a dish cloth and gently pull the sides away from the candle. After a few snapping sounds, they will pop right out.

Why not pair these floating beeswax candles with a bouquet of homegrown flowers? Arrange a few candles in a paper berry box and give with a bouquet of freshly cut flowers tied with ribbon.

Healing Crystals Candle

MAKES ONE 4" TIN CANDLE

These healing candles are like a secret treasure. The silver tin is what you would expect to hold a candle, but once you open up the tin you're greeted with a pretty pink, fragrant candle topped with glittering crystals. There are three wicks in this candle which allows the wide surface to burn evenly.

MATERIALS

- One 4" tin container with lid
- 5 oz (140 g) of soy wax for container candles
- Three HTP 104 - 65 2.5" waxed and wired wicks with tabs
- 0.3 oz (9 ml) vitality blend fragrance or essential oils blend containing Lavender, Lemongrass, Mandarin, Patchouli, Geranium, and Ylang Ylang
- 1" piece of pink crayon
- Assorted crystals

EQUIPMENT

- Double boiler
- Hot glue gun and glue or wax adhesive
- Thermometer
- Sharp scissors
- Kitchen scale
- Paper cup
- Heatproof container with pour spout

Healing Crystals

The crystals used in this project are decorative but if you want to add a special element to this candle, visit a crystal shop and find some healing crystals. Some ideas could be stones associated with relaxation (amethyst), healing (quartz), luck (jade) and success (citrine).

1 Measure and melt the soy wax in a double boiler with a thermometer. While the wax is melting, measure the scent oil into a paper cup.

2 Place the wicks at half the radius of the container, evenly spaced at three points around the base of the candle as if there were three candles set together inside the tin. Attach each of the wicks with wax adhesive or hot glue.

3 When the melted wax has reached the specified temperature for adding dye or scent oil (i.e.: 160°F – see the instructions that came with your wax), add in 1" of pink crayon cut into pieces. Stir well until the color has completely dissolved into the wax.

4 If the wax has cooled, put it back on the heat to bring it up to temperature and add the scent oil. Stir well to ensure the oil is completely mixed into the wax.

5 Cool the wax to 140°F and pour it into the tin around the wicks leaving ¼" of headspace.

Tip

The headspace allows the tin to close even with the crystals in place.

6 Leave the candle untouched to set just enough so that the crystals will not slip down into the wax. The wax should still be slightly warm to the touch; gently press each crystal on the wax surface so that it attaches to the wax. Be careful not to press the crystals too hard, as this can create cracks in the wax surface. Trim wicks to ¼".

The fun of this candle is the secret treasure that is hidden within a silver tin embellished with gold gem stickers. Buy sheets of stickers and customize the pattern for a one-of-a-kind treasure. The tin is gorgeous in its own right but just wait until the lucky recipient opens it and the pops of color and the glittering crystals are unveiled!

Herbal Sleepy Time Wax Melts

MAKES TWENTY-FIVE 0.3 OZ (9 G) WAX MELTS

With busy days and hectic schedules, we could all use a good night's sleep. These herbal chamomile, calendula and lavender wax melts are the perfect way to send you to dreamland, as the calming scent of herbs will fill the room and relax you as the wax melts. Packaged with a wax warmer, they are a lovely self-care package for a friend that could use a restful evening.

MATERIALS

- 8 oz (225g) microwaveable soy wax for wax melts

- 0.5 oz (15 ml) serenity blend fragrance or lavender essential oil

- 1 tbsp each dried lavender buds, chamomile flowers and calendula petals

EQUIPMENT

- Heatproof container with a pour spout

- Microwave

- Kitchen scale

- Paper cup

- Silicone candy/baking /soap mold – flower shape

Sleepy Time Herb Blend

There are some herbs that wake you up and others that quiet you down. Herbs like lavender, chamomile, calendula, hops, mint and passionflower are calming for the nerves and quieting for the mind. Using these herbs before bed can help to promote an easier time falling asleep as well as better quality of sleep.

Making this recipe as herbal wax melts instead of a candle allows the wax, oils and herbs to melt together at a safe temperature without risk that the herbs will catch fire. Of course, never leave a candle burning at bedtime.

This recipe can be made in either a microwave or in a double boiler. The steps to make wax melts in the microwave are outlined here. To make this recipe in a double boiler, use the same materials but follow the instructions and use the equipment in the Citrus Celebration Wax Melts, page 24.

1 Weigh microwaveable soy wax for wax melts in a heatproof container with a pour spout.

2 Weigh scent oil in a paper cup. Prepare the herbs in advance of using the microwave so you are ready to add them as soon as the wax has melted.

3 Melt the wax in 20-second intervals to be sure it melts and doesn't cook. You may be tempted to set the timer for longer than 20 seconds as you will see little change in the wax at first. After a few times, you will see the wax quickly turn from a solid to a liquid. Overheating the wax can cause it to burn and smell terrible, so set 20-second intervals and check the wax frequently.

4 When the wax has fully melted, stir in the scent oil and half of the dried herbs.

5 Pour the wax into a flower-shaped mold. Choose a mold used for soap making or candy making to be sure it can handle the heat of melted wax.

6 Sprinkle the remaining herbs on top of each melt and allow the herbal wax melts to dry completely before popping them out.

Fill a wax-lined window bag with the herbal wax melts and label it with letter stamps. Use floral stamps to further embellish the sack. Place the melts in the bag and move them around so their pretty faces show through the window.

Jam Jar Candle Favors

MAKES TWELVE 3.5 OZ (100 G) CANDLES

These jam jar candles make beautiful, natural gifts, and they're easier to make than you think. So easy that you can produce a lot in a short period of time, making them perfect for wedding favors, a shower gift, or a handmade candle-making bonanza!

MATERIALS

- Twelve 4 oz (125 g) jam jars with canning lids and rings

- 2lbs 10 oz (1200 g) soy wax for container candles

- Twelve HTP 126 4" waxed and wired wicks with tabs

- 2.6 oz (75 ml) fragrance or essential oils for scent (optional)

- Crayon pieces or wax dye for color (optional)

EQUIPMENT

- Double boiler

- Hot glue gun and glue or wax adhesive

- Thermometer

- Sharp scissors

- Kitchen scale

- Chopsticks or clothespins

- Old towel

- Paper cup

- Metal tray

- Heatproof container with pour spout

Tip

Soy wax can be dyed any color you want and takes to fragrance perfectly. Try making a large batch and switching up the scents and colors in different combinations. Soy wax also blends well with beeswax which yields a smooth-textured, light golden, slightly sweet smelling candle that captures the benefits of both soy wax and beeswax.

Fun for Everyone!

This project is suitable for even a beginning crafter. That means it's a great choice if you want to get a group together for a day of candle making, no experience necessary. Imagine a fun afternoon with the bridesmaids making a few dozen candles for an outdoor wedding. Pick your scent to personalize the candles, then dress them up with fabric and cord.

1 Assemble the double boiler and measure wax into the top pot. Heat over medium heat setting, stirring regularly.

2 While the wax is melting, measure scent oil and prepare the crayons or wax dye if using.

3 Prepare the jars by adding a bit of hot glue or wax adhesive to the bottom of the wick tabs and press them firmly into the centers of the jars. Place the jars on a metal tray or pan.

4 If you are adding color and scent, bring the wax to the specified temperature for adding dye or scent oil (i.e.: 160°F – see the instructions that came with your wax). Add color and scent and mix thoroughly to combine.

5 Cool wax to 140°F and carefully pour into jars.

6 Prop up the wicks with chopsticks or clothespins to keep them centered. Wrap a towel around the outside of the tray or pan and set aside to cool. Be careful not to disturb the candles too much while they set. Once set, trim the wicks to ¼" above the wax.

To make these jam jars picture perfect, cut out a circle of fabric that is the diameter of the jar lid. Lay the fabric on the lid and secure the lid to the jar with the ring. Tie a bit of coordinating jute cord around the ring.

Lavender Candle

MAKES ONE 16 OZ (450 G) CANDLE

Lavender is THE herb of relaxation. These pressed herb candles add a beautiful natural look and a heavenly scent that brings peace and serenity to the space. This design uses real herbs pressed on the inside of a glass canning jar to decorate the candle. The wicks are a slightly thinner diameter than would normally be used for a wide mouth jar like this; that way the wax will not burn all the way to the sides of the jar, dislodging the pressed herbs. When the candle has burned all the way to the bottom of the jar, you can add a votive or tea light in its place and continue to enjoy the pressed lavender flowers and leaves on the jar.

MATERIALS

- One 16 oz (475 ml) wide mouth glass canning jar
- 0.6 lb (270 g) soy wax for container candles
- 0.4 lb (180 g) beeswax pastilles
- One HTP 104 6" waxed and wired wick with tab
- 1 oz (30 ml) lavender fragrance or essential oil for scent (optional)
- Pressed young English lavender leaves and flower stems – with leaves and flowers no larger than 1" long and $1/2$" wide (see Step 1)

EQUIPMENT

- Double boiler
- Hot glue gun and glue or wax adhesive
- Thermometer
- Sharp scissors
- Kitchen scale
- Paper cup
- Old towel
- Craft paintbrush
- Chopsticks or clothespins
- Heatproof container with pour spout

Lovely Lavender

Lavender is the herb of relaxation and serenity. It's a heavenly floral scent that helps you to wind down and de-stress. Try lighting one as part of your before bed routine to soothe and relax you – just make sure you blow out the candle before falling into a peaceful slumber.

1 Harvest young lavender flowers and leaves on thin green stems (not the older woody stems with large flowers) and press them between heavy books or with a wooden press for a week, until they are very flat and dry. Cut the lavender stems so they will sit at least 1" below the rim of the jar.

2 Weigh wax and melt in a double boiler with a thermometer attached. Measure the lavender oil in the paper cup and set aside.

3 Dip a pressed lavender bloom in the melted wax. Working quickly, place the stem on the inside of the jar; use the paintbrush to press it firmly in place as the wax cools. Brush melted wax over the lavender stem to hold it in place. Continue to add lavender stems around the inside of the jar, being sure that each is pressed completely flat on the jar.

4 When the lavender appliqués have dried, add a dab of hot glue or wax adhesive to attach the wick to the center bottom of the jar. Prop up the wick with a chopstick or clothespin to keep it centered.

5 If you are adding color and fragrance, bring the wax to the specified temperature for adding dye or scent oil (i.e.: 160°F—see the instructions that came with your wax). Add color and scent and mix thoroughly to combine. Cool wax to 140°F and carefully pour into jars.

6 Wrap a towel around the outside of the jar and set aside to cool. Be careful not to disturb the candle too much while it sets. Once set, trim the wick to $1/4$" above the wax.

Add a lid to the jar and attach a chalkboard label to the top of the lid. Use a chalk marker so the message won't rub off easily (but it will come off with water and a cloth). Practice your script a few times before you add it to the label. Keep in mind that whoever is lucky enough to get this beautiful handmade candle won't be critiquing your handwriting! They will be far too taken with the candle and thoughtful sentiment.

Ombré Evergreen Candle

MAKES ONE 3" (225 G) SQUARE CANDLE

This modern ombré candle subtly nods to the holidays, making it a lovely winter gift idea that doesn't date itself as soon as the festivities are over. The ombré effect is created with just one color of wax dye in different strengths to give the candle a decorative graduated color that adds elegance and interest along with a pop of color while maintaining a minimalist style.

MATERIALS

- One 3" x 3" x 3.5" square glass candle jar

- One wood wick with metal tab

- 0.5 lb (225g) soy wax for container candles

- One green dye chip for candle making (or the appropriate number of chips for 225g of wax)

- 0.5 oz (15 ml) evergreen fragrance or essential oil, divided into thirds

EQUIPMENT

- Double boiler

- Thermometer

- Kitchen scale

- Fine-tip pruning shears to trim wick

- Hot glue gun and glue or wax adhesive

- Rubber gloves

- Old towel

- Heatproof container with pour spout

- Three paper cups or shot glasses

Tip

The active time for this project isn't that much more than other candle-making projects. However, it does take a full day to complete this project because of the time for the wax to harden in between each layer. You can scale this project up or down to have as many layers as you would like, but keep in mind that the candle wax needs to harden completely before you pour the next layer.

Color a Candle for Every Season

This candle has a spruce-inspired blue-green color that adds a modern touch to winter celebrations, but an ombré candle project can be done at any time of the year. Change it up depending on the season. For the spring, use pretty pastels. For summer, use bold jewel tones. And for fall, use warm colors like yellow, orange and red. You can also swap out the fragrance to match the seasonal colors.

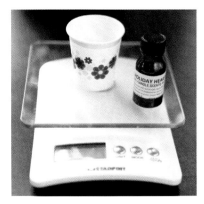

1 Weigh the soy wax and add it to a double boiler on medium heat. While the wax is melting, measure the fragrance or essential oil into three paper cups equally. Then prepare the dye chips.

2 Prepare the wood wick by determining its final height in the candle, ¹/₄" above the top of the wax. Feed the wooden wick into the metal base and use a dab of hot glue or wax adhesive to attach it to the bottom of the jar at the center.

3 Prepare your ombré colors by calculating how much dye will be needed for the amount of wax. Then, divide the dye chip into three pieces: one large, one medium and one small. The larger the difference between the sizes of the chips will mean a greater difference in the color of each wax layer. Use rubber gloves to protect your hands from the dye while you're cutting the chip.

4 Add each piece of dye chip to a shot glass and top with hot wax. Use a chopstick to stir and dissolve the dye chip completely. If the dye chip doesn't completely dissolve, you can place the shot glass in the double boiler to heat it up a bit more.

5 When the melted wax has reached the specified temperature for adding dye or scent oil (i.e.: 160°F – see the instructions that came with your wax), pour a third of the wax into a heatproof measuring cup, add the wax you dissolved the largest dye chip in and pour in one third of the scent oil. Stir well to combine.

6 Cool wax to 140°F and pour into the jar. Leave it untouched to set for at least one hour. It could take longer than an hour for the wax layer to set, depending on the temperature in the room that you're working in.

Tips

- You can trim the candle wick after the candle is poured, but you'll get a cleaner cut if you measure and trim the wick before you pour the candle.

- When using a wood wick and a square jar, align the wick so that it is centered within the square.

7 Follow Step 5–6 for the remaining two layers, adding the scent oil and the wax with the dissolved medium chip first and then the wax with the dissolved small chip. Pour each layer only when the previous layer is completely set.

Wrap the candle with a piece of jute twine and insert a freshly cut sprig of evergreen between the bow and the candle glass. The simple and natural wrapping allows for the gorgeous ombré to peek through, ready to be revealed completely when the twine has been removed.

Pumpkin Spice Candle

MAKES ONE 8 OZ (225 G) CANDLE

This candle project is meant to be used soon after it is made because the container is a real pumpkin, and therefore perishable. There are a whole host of wonderful natural containers like citrus rinds, apples, gourds, and pumpkins that can be used to make a container candle.

MATERIALS

- One miniature pumpkin, approximately 6" in diameter

- Wired and waxed wick with tab

- 8 oz (225 g) of soy wax for container candles

- 0.8 oz (24 ml) of pumpkin spice fragrance or essential oil blend

EQUIPMENT

- Paring knife

- Tablespoon or melon baller

- Double boiler

- Thermometer

- Sharp scissors

- Kitchen scale

- Old towel

- Paper cup

- Chopsticks or clothespins

- Heatproof container with pour spout

Tip

When using perishables as candle containers, it's best to choose the fruits before they completely ripen, so they last the longest time possible after pouring the candle. Make the candle just before it is meant to be given as a gift or used at a party. The wax will seal the open flesh and prevent some of the decomposition. Use a wood slice or a plate under the candle to protect the surface below and never leave a burning candle unattended.

Warm Up with Spice

The warm notes of cinnamon, ginger, nutmeg, clove, cardamom and vanilla are perfect for the fall. They fill the house with coziness and allow you to settle into shorter days and longer nights. It's a scent combination that doesn't feel as comfortable in the spring and summer, so enjoy it while you can. Pumpkin spice is a celebration that is meant to be enjoyed before the season passes.

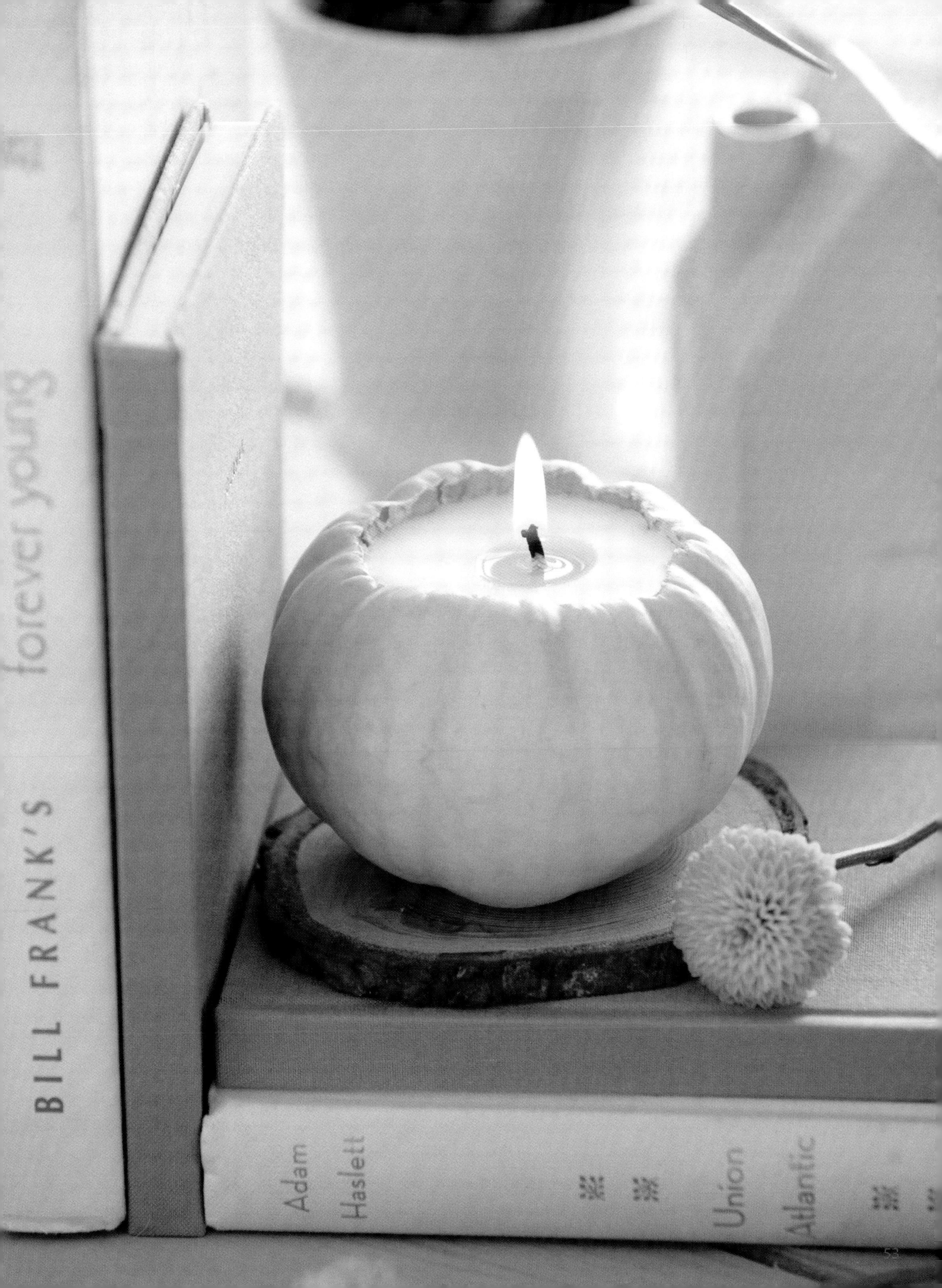
BILL FRANK'S
forever young
Adam
Haslett
Union
Atlantic

MAKE IT! • PUMPKIN SPICE CANDLE

1 Prepare the pumpkin as if you were making a small jack-o-lantern: use a paring knife to cut into the pumpkin and remove the top; then use a tablespoon or melon baller to scrape out the seeds and fibers.

2 Weigh the soy wax and add it to a double boiler on medium heat.

3 When the melted wax has reached the specified temperature for adding scent oil (i.e.: 160°F – see the instructions that came with your wax), add the scent oil. Stir well to bind.

4 Cool the wax to 140°F and pour it into the pumpkin.

5 When the candle wax starts to turn opaque, insert the wick. Use chopsticks to hold the wick in place as the candle cools. Wrap the candle in a towel and place it in a warm room to slowly set.

6 Allow the candle to cure for 24 hours undisturbed. Once cured, trim the wick with scissors to 1/4" above the surface of the wax.

This gift is best made the day before it is intended to be given as a gift and with the understanding that the recipient will use it soon after receiving it. Place the pumpkin on a wood slice or a pretty ceramic plate and wrap it with a linen ribbon. Attach a sweet little tag with coordinating baker's twine.

Seashell Tea Lights

MAKES SIX 0.6 OZ (18 G) TEA LIGHTS

Beach lovers will enjoy these delightful beeswax seashell candles, which look right at home in a shallow vessel filled with sand or grouped in the center of a table with sea glass and other beachcombed objects scattered around them.

MATERIALS

- 4 oz (115 g) of beeswax

- Eight medium-sized clam or oyster shells, deep enough to hold the same amount of wax as a standard tea light

- Eight waxed and wired 1" tea light wicks with tabs

- Sand

EQUIPMENT

- Double boiler

- Kitchen scale

- Plastic tray/container to hold shells while pouring wax and candles are setting up

- Heatproof container with pour spout

Memories of the Sea

Seashell tea lights are a wonderful way to create mementos of special trips to the beach, vacations by the ocean or add to a beach-themed décor. And seashells are widely available. If you don't live near a beach where you can collect shells, you will easily find a huge selection at craft stores, along with the white sand and lots of containers that can be used for display.

MAKE IT! • SEASHELL TEA LIGHTS

1 Prepare the seashells by washing and drying them thoroughly.

2 Place the shells in a plastic tray filled with sand to hold them in place for pouring the wax. The sand will keep the shells in place while the wax sets.

3 Melt the beeswax in a double boiler. Keep a close watch on it so that it can be poured as soon as it's completely liquid.

4 Carefully pour wax into the shells, making sure that they stay level and wax doesn't spill over the edges. As the wax starts to cool and turn opaque around the edges, place a wick in the center of each one. The wicks are short and should easily stay in place.

5 Let the seashell tea lights cool and cure for 24 hours undisturbed.

A small bucket, reminiscent of a sand pail, will contain all of the seashell tea lights.
A simple ribbon and tag make gift giving beautiful (and easy!).

Wine & Roses Sand Candle

MAKES ONE 10.5 OZ (300 G) CANDLE

This beautiful candle has layers of wine- and rose-colored granulated paraffin wax sand that you simply scent and then pour in layers into a stemless wine glass. When the candle top is sealed, the wax will not spill and you can confidently transport the candle for gift giving. Making a sand art candle like this is a fun project to do with children, as it doesn't require melting the wax before pouring the candle. It's also a fantastic project for an adult crafting night accompanied by, you guessed it, wine.

MATERIALS

- Thick-walled stemless wine glass

- LX18-150 6" waxed and wired paraffin wick with tab

- 10.5 oz (300 g) granulated wax in wine, burgundy, rose, and white

- 0.2 oz (5 ml) floral fragrance oil or essential oil blend that includes rose

EQUIPMENT

- Double boiler

- Hot glue gun and glue or wax adhesive

- Sharp scissors

- Large disposable paper cups

- Heatproof container with pour spout

Modern Roses

Roses used to be thought of as old-fashioned flowers, and while they have a prominent place in the history books, roses are resurfacing as a modern herb. The petals are edible, the oil is a powerful skin elixir and even the rose hips that are left behind when the petals fall are full of vitamins and antioxidants. The traditional scent of rose may remind you of your grandmother, but it's time to give it another chance. Rose is the scent of romance, after all!

MAKE IT! • WINE & ROSES SAND CANDLE

1 Prepare the wine glass by gluing the wick into the bottom of the glass at the center.

2 Pour the different colors of granulated wax into paper cups and stir in a few drops of fragrance oil to add scent to the candle. Be careful not to add too much scent oil to prevent the wax from clumping.

3 Bend the mouth of the paper cup to create a pour spout and pour one color of the wax granules into the wine glass, covering the wick base; pour until you get the thickness that you like for the first layer.

4 Add subsequent layers in varying colors to achieve a desirable pattern. Tilting the jar and adding the wax at angles produces some beautiful patterns. Pushing down the sides with a chopstick can also create a unique pattern. Have fun and play with the design. Stop adding wax when there you are 1" from the top of the wine glass.

5 To seal the candle in place, melt a small amount of paraffin granules in the canning jar or a shot glass set in a pan of water to make a double boiler.

6 Add a few drops of fragrance oil to the wax and pour it on to the top of the candle to completely cover the exposed granules and spread to the sides of the glass.